Foreword

n his sermon at World Youth Day 2008
pilgrims that it is important that each o … p
with him and allow ourselves to be gui … ner
nvited those present to ask themselve …
Yet the question is not just for the you … Holy
Spirit 'needs to be constantly reawaker
People of God'. (*Dominum et vivificant* …

In the Creed we proclaim our belief in the Holy Spirit 'the Lord and giver of life, who proceeds from the Father and the Son'. But have we really taken the time or trouble to understand what we say, or the Holy Spirit of whom we speak? This season's resource for small group and individual reflection is an opportunity for each of us to seize upon Pope Benedict's invitation to know the Holy Spirit and, more than this, to welcome the Holy Spirit as 'the guide of our souls'.

It is the Holy Spirit, the Lord, the giver of life, who has fashioned everything that is; the breath of God that brings all things to life. Be open to his work in you, that you may be drawn more fully into the life and love of the Trinity. Be open to his work in you, that the parishes in which you live and worship may be beacons of joy and hope. Be open to him, that you may be everything the Father intended you to be; the glory of God, people fully alive.

May the Holy Spirit who makes all things new live in your hearts and minds.

With my blessing and prayers

+ Cormac Murphy-O'Connor

Cardinal Cormac Murphy-O'Connor
Archbishop of Westminster

About this Book

Lord, Giver of Life is an opportunity for us to reflect on the third person of the Trinity, the Holy Spirit. Over the course of 42 daily meditations and 6 sessions for small groups, we hope that you will come to a fuller understanding of the Spirit and through him deepen your relationship with God the Father and his Son Jesus Christ.

Each of the six weeks has a different theme. Week One looks at the Holy Spirit in the life of Christ while Week Two considers the Spirit in the life of Christ's bride, the Church. Week Three considers the Holy Spirit in our own lives as individuals and Week Four looks at the Spirit in the lives of four New Testament figures. In Week Five we will look at the gifts of the Holy Spirit. During Holy Week we will look at the fruits of the Holy Spirit, asking what a life lived in the Spirit looks like. We will also reflect on Christ's passion and death, reflecting on the Spirit's work at the heart of the paschal mystery.

The format of this booklet is unchanged from previous ones in the *exploring faith* series. The group sessions are intended as a guide and facilitators should feel free to add to them where necessary according to the mood and needs of the group. That said, the basic format is such that the session could be taken and followed with little or no embellishment. The daily meditations for Saturday and Sunday draw on the Sunday readings and will help us to prepare for our Sunday celebration of the Mass.

At Mass, the readings you hear are taken from the *Jerusalem Bible* translation except the Psalms which come from the *Grail* translation. In this booklet we have chosen to provide the translation found in the *New Revised Standard Version* of the Bible.

The Old Testament proclaimed the Father clearly, but the Son more obscurely. The New Testament revealed the Son and gave us a glimpse of the divinity of the Spirit. Now the Spirit dwells among us and grants us a clearer vision of himself… By advancing and progressing 'from glory to glory,' the light of the Trinity will shine in ever more brilliant rays.

St. Gregory of Nazianzus, also known as the Theologian

Group Session One

Opening Prayer

A: Bless the Lord, O my soul.
You stretch out the heavens like a tent.
You set the earth on its foundations.
You cover it with the deep as with a garment.

B: You make springs gush forth in the valleys.
You cause the grass to grow for the cattle,
and plants for people to use,
to bring forth food from the earth,
and wine to gladden the human heart.

A: O Lord, how manifold are your works!
In wisdom you have made them all;
the earth is full of your creatures,
living things both great and small.

B: When you open your hand they are filled with good things
when you hide your face, they are dismayed;
when you take away their breath, they die
when you send forth your spirit they are created;
and you renew the face of the ground.

From Psalm 103 (104)

All: Glory be…

Come, Holy Spirit, fill the hearts of your faithful
and kindle in them the fire of your love.
Send forth your spirit and they shall be created
and you will renew the face of the earth.

See Psalm 103:30 and Gospel Acclamation for Pentecost

Let us listen carefully to the Word of the Lord,
and attend to it with the ear of our hearts.
Let us welcome it, and faithfully put it into practice.

St. Benedict of Nursia (c.480-c.547) adapted

Explore the Scriptures *Romans 8:6-11*

To set the mind on the flesh is death, but to set the mind on the Spirit is life and peace. For this reason the mind that is set on the flesh is hostile to God; it does not submit to God's law—indeed it cannot, and those who are in the flesh cannot please God.

But you are not in the flesh; you are in the Spirit, since the Spirit of God dwells in you. Anyone who does not have the Spirit of Christ does not belong to him. But if Christ is in you, though the body is dead because of sin, the spirit is life because of righteousness. If the Spirit of him who raised Jesus from the dead dwells in you, he who raised Christ from the dead will give life to your mortal bodies also through his Spirit that dwells in you.

Before the passage is read again with a different voice you may wish to share a word, an image or a phrase that has struck you. These thoughts can be discussed further after the second reading.

Reflection

'We believe in the Holy Spirit, the Lord, the giver of life'. In 1986 Pope John Paul II issued his encyclical, *Dominum et vivificantem* (Lord, Giver of Life), on the Holy Spirit in the Life of the Church and the World. Introducing this letter he said that our faith in the Holy Spirit as the giver of life needs to be 'constantly reawakened and deepened'.

In the Scriptures the Holy Spirit is presented as a creative or life giving force. At the dawn of creation the Holy Spirit is found hovering over the waters (Genesis 1:2). Indeed he is not only present at the moment of creation, he is present in that creation, making men and women in his own image. It is he, the breath of God that breathes life into humankind (Genesis 2:7). Again, it is the Holy Spirit, the giver of life, that overshadows Mary at the incarnation, when Christ was begotten and whose outpouring at Pentecost galvanises the apostles into action, announcing the birth of the Church.

In the above passage from the letter to the Romans St. Paul reminds us that this same Spirit is alive in each of us. 'But you are not in the flesh', he says, 'you are in the Spirit, since the Spirit of God dwells in you'. It is this Holy Spirit at work in us 'that gives life' (John 6:63). For the Samaritan Woman, it promises to be, as Christ puts it, 'a spring of water gushing up to eternal life' (John 4:14), for those born of water and the Spirit it is the key to the kingdom of God (John 3:5).

St. Paul says that the spirit is life because of righteousness. What does he mean? For St. Paul righteousness – being right with God – has been made possible by Christ. In his living, dying and rising again Christ, who was one with the Spirit, has triumphed over sin and death, overcoming the gulf or barriers that human sin has erected between us and God. Those barriers have their origins in the Fall, when we turned away from God and the gracious working of the Holy Spirit that hovered over the waters and brought us to life. With these barriers gone the Holy Spirit can commence its life giving work once more; a work that draws us closer to the Father and through which he reveals or communicates himself. It is for this reason that the waters of baptism are said to make 'an end of sin and a new beginning of goodness' and that Christ says that the Holy Spirit will only come when his own work has been accomplished (John 16:7).

How conscious have I been of the Holy Spirit being at work in my life? What image of the Holy Spirit does today's Scripture passage and reflection bring to mind? How has today's session impacted on my understanding of the Holy Spirit? What fresh insight has it given me?

From Dominum et vivificantem

13. It seems then that even the words spoken by Jesus in the farewell discourse should be read again in the light of that 'beginning,' so long ago yet fundamental, which we know from Genesis. 'If I do not go away, the Counsellor will not come to you; but if I go, I will send him to you.' Describing his 'departure' *as a condition* for the 'coming' of the Counsellor, Christ links the new beginning of God's salvific self-communication in the Holy Spirit with the mystery of the Redemption. It is a new beginning, first of all because *between* the first beginning and the whole of human history – from the original fall onwards – *sin has intervened*, sin which is in contradiction to the presence of the Spirit of God in creation, and which is above all in *contradiction to God's salvific self-communication to man.*

Leader: Aloud or in the silence of our hearts let us bring to the Father our thanks (pause)…

Leader: In sorrow let us ask the Father for forgiveness (pause)…

Leader: With confidence let us entrust to the Father our cares and concerns (pause)…

Closing Prayer

Heavenly King,
Consoler Spirit,
Spirit of Truth,
present everywhere and filling all things,
treasure of all good and Source of all life,
come dwell in us,
cleanse and save us,
You who are All Good!

Byzantine Liturgy, Pentecost Vespers, Troparion

Today's Second Reading *1 Peter 3:18-22 (NRSV translation)*

For Christ also suffered for sins once for all, the righteous for the unrighteous, in order to bring you to God. He was put to death in the flesh, but made alive in the spirit, in which also he went and made a proclamation to the spirits in prison, who in former times did not obey, when God waited patiently in the days of Noah, during the building of the ark, in which a few, that is, eight people, were saved through water. And baptism, which this prefigured, now saves you—not as a removal of dirt from the body, but as an appeal to God for a good conscience, through the resurrection of Jesus Christ, who has gone into heaven and is at the right hand of God, with angels, authorities, and powers made subject to him.

Have you stopped to consider what a blessing your baptism is, what a remarkable thing has been done for and to you? The Holy Spirit is with us to guide us and help us to appreciate the life, message and mission of Christ. Over the next six weeks we will consider how he does this and pray that we may open ourselves to his loving action.

Breathe in me, O Holy Spirit,
that my thoughts may all be holy.
Act in me, O Holy Spirit,
that my work, too, may be holy.
Draw my heart, O Holy Spirit,
that I love but what is holy.
Strengthen me, O Holy Spirit,
to defend all that is holy.
Guard me, then, O Holy Spirit,
that I always may be holy.
Amen.

St. Augustine (354-430)

Sharing in Christ's Mission

When the Spirit of truth comes, he will guide you into all the truth; for he will not speak on his own, but will speak whatever he hears, and he will declare to you the things that are to come. He will glorify me, because he will take what is mine and declare it to you.

John 16:13-14

Towards the end of his earthly ministry Jesus promised that his followers would not be orphaned by his departure, but that another advocate, the Holy Spirit, would continue his work and presence among them, taking from what is his (Christ's) and declaring it to them. Nonetheless, the Spirit's continuation of Christ's work is not to be understood in the same terms as a relay race, with one person holding and then passing on the baton to someone else, as if there were ever a time when Christ's life and ministry was lived and exercised independently of the Holy Spirit. As the *Catechism* reminds us, 'Christ's whole work is in fact a joint mission of the Son and Holy Spirit' (CCC, 727).

How do I see myself sharing in Christ's Mission?

Holy Spirit, Lord of Light.
From the clear celestial height,
Thy pure beaming radiance give.

Come, thou father of the poor,
Come with treasures which endure,
Come, thou light of all that live.

From the Pentecost Sequence

Conceived by the power of the Holy Spirit

In the beginning was the Word, and the Word was with God, and the Word was God… the Word became flesh and lived among us…

John 1:1, 14

The whole of scripture recounts the story of a God who desires that we should know him, not a distant God, but a God willing to reveal himself to us. At the dawn of creation, we learn of a God who creates from nothing not because he needs to create, but because he loves. God so loved us that he sent his only Son. In Christ the divine and the human meet, the Word - God - becomes flesh, and lives among us. This union between the human and divine was the work of the Holy Spirit. 'How can this be, since I am a virgin?' asked Mary, and the Angel replied, 'The Holy Spirit will come upon you, and the power of the Most High will overshadow you; therefore the child to be born will be holy; he will be called Son of God' *(Luke 1:34, 35)*.

Thou, of all consolers best,
Thou, the soul's delightful guest,
Dost refreshing peace bestow.

Thou in toil art comfort sweet,
Pleasant coolness in the heat,
Solace in the midst of woe.

From the Pentecost Sequence

Anointed by the Holy Spirit

And John (the Baptist) testified, 'I saw the Spirit descending from heaven like a dove, and it remained on him. I myself did not know him, but the one who sent me to baptise with water said to me, 'He on whom you see the Spirit descend and remain is the one who baptises with the Holy Spirit.'

John 1:32-33

Following his baptism in the Jordan, Jesus was publicly revealed as the Messiah, the Christ or the Anointed One upon whom, as Isaiah foretold, the Spirit of the Lord would come to rest (Isaiah 11:2). Of course the Holy Spirit can be found at work in others. In the prophets who have spoken at his prompting, in Simeon who recognised in Christ the salvation prepared for all nations, in Mary who, as we shall reflect, was prepared by the Spirit. Yet Christ, as the account of his baptism recalls, was the Son of God, on whom the Holy Spirit not merely descended but remained permanently, i.e. he possessed the fullness of the Holy Spirit, possessing the fullness of the Holy Spirit. This manifests itself in what he accomplishes – salvation for the broken hearted, the captive – and his ability, as John relates in this passage, to give or impart the Holy Spirit.

Light immortal, light divine,
Visit thou these hearts of thine
And our inmost being fill.

If thou take thy grace away,
Nothing pure in man will stay;
All his good is turned to ill.

From the Pentecost Sequence

Led by the Spirit

Jesus, full of the Holy Spirit, returned from the Jordan and was led by the Spirit in the wilderness, where for forty days he was tempted by the devil.

Luke 4:1-2

In Scripture the Holy Spirit is frequently experienced as a nudging, gentle force, guiding us to God. Thus, in 1 Kings (19:11-13), Elijah perceives the Lord's presence in the gentle breeze rather than the windstorm, earthquake or fire that preceded it. The term 'Spirit' translates from the Hebrew word ruah, which, in its main sense, means breath, air, wind, something gentle. However, in the different accounts of his temptation in the desert Jesus is variously 'led' (Matthew 4:1, Luke 4:1) or 'driven out' (Mark 1:12) into the wilderness by the Holy Spirit.

Some people have a live sense of their being touched, called, led or driven by the Holy Spirit. Reflecting on your own experiences, how would you describe the Holy Spirit's action in your life?

Heal our wounds, our strength renew;
On our dryness pour thy dew;
Wash the stains of guilt away.

Bend the stubborn heart and will,
Melt the frozen, warm the chill,
Guide the steps that go astray.

From the Pentecost Sequence

The two hands of the Father

But if it is by the finger of God that I cast out the demons, then the kingdom of God has come to you.

Luke 11:20

These words form part of Christ's response to those who suggested that his curing of a possessed mute was accomplished by Beelzebul 'the ruler of the demons'. Matthew's Gospel also recounts this episode and Christ's response, but translates 'finger of God' as 'Spirit of God'. 'But', says Matthew's Gospel, 'if it is by the Spirit of God that I cast out demons, then the kingdom of God has come to you' (12:28). The finger of God is also identified with the work of the Spirit by the psalmist who describes the heavens, moon and stars, as the work of God's fingers (Psalm 8:3). These same themes are pursued by St. Irenaeus, the second century bishop of Lyons, when he speaks of humankind's being fashioned by the Son and Spirit, the 'hands of God'. In today's passage, Christ testifies to his working with the Spirit in establishing God's reign.

Thou, on those who evermore,
Thee confess and thee adore,
In thy sevenfold gifts descend.

Give us comfort when we die;
Give us life with thee on high;
Give us joys that never end.

From the Pentecost Sequence

Tomorrow's Second Reading *Romans 8:31-34 (NRSV translation)*

If God is for us, who is against us? He who did not withhold his own Son, but gave him up for all of us, will he not with him also give us everything else? Who will bring any charge against God's elect? It is God who justifies. Who is to condemn? It is Christ Jesus, who died, yes, who was raised, who is at the right hand of God, who indeed intercedes for us.

This passage from St. Paul's letter to the Romans logically follows the Old Testament reading for the day – the Genesis account of God putting Abraham to the test by asking him to sacrifice his son Isaac. God abhors the death of any human yet is willing to offer up his Son for our faults and failings, a message St. Paul was keen to preach to the Roman church (Romans 15:20). This letter came at a time when Paul's travels were coming to a close and was therefore an opportunity to present his missionary reflections on salvation and God's love offered to all through faith in Christ Jesus.

Lord our God,
you renew us with food from heaven;
fill our hearts with the gentle love of your Spirit.
May the gifts we have received in this life
lead us to the gift of eternal joy.
We ask this through Christ our Lord.

Prayer after communion, Votive Mass for the Holy Spirit

Group Session Two

Opening Prayer

A: I bow down toward your holy temple
and give thanks to your name
for your steadfast love and your faithfulness;

B: For you have exalted your name
and your word above everything…

A: All the kings of the earth shall praise you, O Lord
for they have heard the words of your mouth.

B: They shall sing of the ways of the Lord,
for great is the glory of the Lord.

A: For though the Lord is high, he regards the lowly;
but the haughty he perceives from far away.

All: Glory be…

From Psalm 137 (138)

Come, Holy Spirit, fill the hearts of your faithful
and kindle in them the fire of your love.
Send forth your spirit and they shall be created
and you will renew the face of the earth.

See Psalm 103:30 and Gospel Acclamation for Pentecost

Let us listen carefully to the Word of the Lord,
and attend to it with the ear of our hearts.
Let us welcome it, and faithfully put it into practice.

St. Benedict of Nursia (c.480-c.547) adapted

Explore the Scriptures *Acts 2:1-4, 38, 43-47*

When the day of Pentecost had come, they were all together in one place. And suddenly from heaven there came a sound like the rush of a violent wind, and it filled the entire house where they were sitting. Divided tongues, as of fire, appeared among them, and a tongue rested on each of them. All of them were filled with the Holy Spirit and began to speak in other languages, as the Spirit gave them ability. Peter said to them, 'Repent, and be baptized every one of you in the name of Jesus Christ so that your sins may be forgiven; and you will receive the gift of the Holy Spirit.

Awe came upon everyone, because many wonders and signs were being done by the apostles. All who believed were together and had all things in common; they would sell their possessions and goods and distribute the proceeds to all, as any had need. Day by day, as they spent much time together in the temple, they broke bread at home and ate their food with glad and generous hearts, praising God and having the goodwill of all the people. And day by day the Lord added to their number those who were being saved.

Before the passage is read again with a different voice you may wish to share a word, an image or a phrase that has struck you. These thoughts can be discussed further after the second reading.

Reflection

So often we can think of the Church as a large organisation, riddled with politics and rivalry. What is frequently neglected is the simple fact that our Church is filled with and professes belief in the same Spirit that came to the apostles on the day of Pentecost. This is the same Spirit promised by Christ – the Spirit with whom he had been intimately connected for all eternity. Invocation of the Spirit takes place on a daily basis in the sacramental and liturgical life of the Church. Every time the Eucharist is celebrated the Holy Spirit is invoked by the celebrant upon the gifts of bread and wine placed on the altar. It is the same Spirit who gathers the faithful 'into one body'. At baptism and confirmation, the Spirit is called upon to dwell in the one receiving the sacrament, strengthening what virtues he or she has and aiding his or her sanctification (1 Corinthians 6:19). For this session, reflect as a group on the following 7th century prayer by St. Isidore of Seville, composed for the Synod of Seville in AD 619 and which was used before every session of the Second Vatican Council:

Group Session Two

We stand before you, Holy Spirit,
conscious of our sinfulness, but aware that we gather in your name.
Come to us, remain with us, and enlighten our hearts.
Give us light and strength to know your will,
to make it our own, and to live it in our lives.
Guide us by your wisdom, support us by your power,
for you are God, sharing the glory of Father and Son.
You desire justice for all; enable us to uphold the rights of others;
do not allow us to be misled by ignorance
or corrupted by fear or favour.
Unite us to yourself in the bond of love
and keep us faithful to all that is true.
As we gather in your name, may we temper justice with love,
so that all our discussions and reflections
may be pleasing to you, and earn the reward
promised to good and faithful servants.
We ask this of You who live and reign with the
Father and the Son, one God, for ever and ever. Amen.

Human weakness is a simple fact; we fail and are conscious of that. Even the greatest among us are not immune from sin. St. Peter, one of the great saints and the first pope, the rock on which the Church was built, is recorded in the gospels as having denied Christ three times. Over the centuries many charges have been levelled at the Church, yet we believe that through everything the Holy Spirit is guiding the Church, preserving her from error. The essence of the Church has remained intact, immune from abuse and scandal. As the Holy Spirit binds us in 'wonderful communion' so it is with truth, not allowing Christ's Church to neglect the challenge of Christ's mission or to fall from the truth that he has given us.

Where do we invoke the Spirit? Are we conscious of the Spirit in this group, in ourselves, in the Church?

Leader: Aloud or in the silence of our hearts let us bring to the Father our thanks (pause)…

Leader: In sorrow let us ask the Father for forgiveness (pause)…

Leader: With confidence let us entrust to the Father our cares and concerns (pause)…

Closing Prayer

Heavenly King,
Consoler Spirit,
Spirit of Truth,
present everywhere and filling all things,
treasure of all good and Source of all life,
come dwell in us,
cleanse and save us,
You who are All Good!

Byzantine Liturgy, Pentecost Vespers, Troparion

Today's Second Reading *Romans 8:31-34 (NRSV translation)*

If God is for us, who is against us? He who did not withhold his own Son, but gave him up for all of us, will he not with him also give us everything else? Who will bring any charge against God's elect? It is God who justifies. Who is to condemn? It is Christ Jesus, who died, yes, who was raised, who is at the right hand of God, who indeed intercedes for us.

As Christians it may appear as though we are constantly having to justify ourselves to the secular world. When in the last year have I had to fight the corner for the faith? How conscious am I that it is God not the world who 'justifies'? Do I have an appreciation of Christ's intercession for me at the right hand of the Father?

Breathe in me, O Holy Spirit,
that my thoughts may all be holy.
Act in me, O Holy Spirit,
that my work, too, may be holy.
Draw my heart, O Holy Spirit,
that I love but what is holy.
Strengthen me, O Holy Spirit,
to defend all that is holy.
Guard me, then, O Holy Spirit,
that I always may be holy.
Amen.

St. Augustine (354-430)

Birth of the Church

The earth was a formless void and darkness covered the face of the deep, while a wind from God swept over the face of the waters.

Genesis 1:2

We read in the second chapter of Genesis of the Holy Spirit, 'the breath of God', busy in the act of creation. At the moment of birth the first thing we hope to hear is the cry or breath of an infant, at death we draw our last breath. The Holy Spirit instils us all with life. At Pentecost, the Holy Spirit breathed life into the Church. A small group of fearful followers huddled in a room soon found themselves standing on street corners proclaiming the Risen Lord. Fear was overcome and followers of Christ were drawn together from all corners of the globe. It is the Holy Spirit who brings about this wonderful communion of the faithful. (*Unitatis Redintegratio*, 2).

How open am I to the idea of a transforming Spirit?

From Lumen Gentium

4. When the work which the Father gave the Son to do on earth was accomplished, the Holy Spirit was sent on the day of Pentecost in order that He might continually sanctify the Church, and thus, all those who believe would have access through Christ in one Spirit to the Father... The Spirit dwells in the Church and in the hearts of the faithful, as in a temple.

Creator Spirit, come and visit the souls that are yours
fill with heavenly grace the hearts that you created.
Amen.

Invocation of the Spirit

For the promise is for you, for your children, and for all who are far away, everyone whom the Lord our God calls to him.

Acts 2:39

At key moments in life there are certain things and people we can rely on. Guidance and help from family and friends, solace in a favourite book or song. At the key moments in the life of the Church, she turns to the Holy Spirit. At the opening of each session of the Second Vatican Council a prayer to the Holy Spirit was intoned; on the death of John Paul II Votive Masses to the Holy Spirit were celebrated petitioning the Spirit for wisdom and guidance. The Holy Spirit that came to Peter when he addressed the Sanhedrin (Acts 4:8) is the same Spirit that has been promised to us as a guide and, quite rightly, the Church relies on his intercession.

From Dominum et vivificantem

66. In the midst of the problems, disappointments and hopes, desertions and returns of these times of ours, *the Church* remains *faithful to the mystery of her birth*... Spiritually the event of Pentecost does not belong only to the past: the Church is always in the Upper Room that she bears in her heart.

Father in Heaven...
see your people gathered in prayer,
open to receive the Spirit's flame.
May it come to rest in our hearts
and disperse the divisions of word and tongue.
With one voice and one song
may we praise your name in joy and thanksgiving.
Grant this through Christ our Lord.
Amen.

Alternative Opening Prayer, Vigil Mass, Pentecost Sunday

Unity

Because the spirit of the Lord has filled the world, and that which holds all things together knows what is said.

Wisdom 1:7

Over sixteen centuries ago St. Gregory of Nazianzus told those approaching baptism for the first time that the faith that we profess is of 'one divinity and power, existing one in three, and containing the three in a distinct way'. The very expression of communion that we recall in making the sign of the Cross is present in the Church. Each time we bless ourselves with holy water from the stoup, at the beginning and end of Mass, and when we pray in private, we accept the Trinity as 'companion and patron of our lives'. Not only do we have the mutual support of our brothers and sisters but God's own Spirit who, during the flight from Egypt, came upon seventy of the Israelite elders to 'share the burden' in the wilderness of Sinai (Numbers 11:17, 25). The Spirit that has filled the world binds us together.

Come, Holy Spirit, live in us
with God the Father and the Son,
and grant us your abundant grace
to sanctify and make us one.

Hymn, Divine Office, Prayer during the day, Week 2

Truth

When the Spirit of truth comes, he will guide you into all the truth; for he will not speak on his own, but will speak whatever he hears, and he will declare to you the things that are to come. He will glorify me, because he will take what is mine and declare it to you.

John 16:13-14

Much has been written and said about the incomprehensibility of God. Yet, what our minds cannot comprehend is fully understood by the Spirit who 'searches everything, even the depths of God' (1 Corinthians 2:7-10). However, St. Paul writes in his first letter to the Corinthians that the apostles were able to 'speak God's wisdom, secret and hidden'. This can only have been possible with the power of the Holy Spirit who takes us into the very heart of God and reveals the truth about Jesus, 'the supreme and most complete revelation of God to humanity' (*Dominum et vivificantem,* 5).

From Dominum et vivificantem

4. The Holy Spirit will be the Counsellor of the apostles and the Church, always present in their midst – even though invisible – as the teacher of the same Good News that Christ proclaimed... The Holy Spirit, then, will ensure that in the Church there will always continue *the same truth* which the apostles heard from their Master.

Holy Spirit, come into my heart;
draw it to Thee by Thy power, O my God,
and grant me charity with filial fear.
Preserve me, O ineffable Love, from every evil thought;
warm me, inflame me with Thy dear love,
and every pain will seem light to me.

St. Catherine of Siena (1347-1380)

Unfolding revelation

He said to them, 'But who do you say that I am?' Simon Peter answered, 'You are the Messiah, the Son of the living God.' And Jesus answered him, 'Blessed are you, Simon son of Jonah! For flesh and blood has not revealed this to you, but my Father in heaven.

Matthew 16:16-17

In his book, *The Creed in the Catechism*, Eamon Duffy writes that we are in the 'epoch of unfolding'. This 'unfolding' or unpacking of the revelation of Christ is not possible without the Spirit and properly understood it is a communal and ecclesial act. As individuals we can fall prey to arbitrariness or fanaticism – in our interpretation of Christ's message and the words we inherit – but the Spirit guides us through the community to the truth. When St. Paul writes that the mystery of Christ was 'hidden throughout the ages and generations but has now been revealed to his saints' (Colossians 1.26), he pointedly remarks that this revelation comes through the Spirit, and is given to a group, to the Church.

Lord, my God,
You who are the source of all good,
help me to be aware that I owe this to you,
as the chief duty of my life,
that my every word and thought may speak of you.
Amen.

Adapted from a sermon 'On the Trinity' by St. Hilary of Poitiers (c.315–368)

Tomorrow's Second Reading *I Corinthians 1:22-25 (NRSV translation)*

For Jews demand signs and Greeks desire wisdom, but we proclaim Christ crucified, a stumbling-block to Jews and foolishness to Gentiles, but to those who are the called, both Jews and Greeks, Christ the power of God and the wisdom of God. For God's foolishness is wiser than human wisdom, and God's weakness is stronger than human strength.

Written from Ephesus, Paul's first letter to the Corinthians was a reaction to a request for advice on a series of problems which faced the community. The community itself was mixed with both Jews and pagans and people from all walks of life. Not surprisingly the difficulties that Paul was presented with were diverse. St. Paul in this passage talks of a suffering Messiah, a thought unthinkable to both the Jews, who anticipated a powerful king, and to the Greeks accustomed to haughty and capricious 'gods'. He reminds the community that Christ is the unifying force who, in his love for God, went to his death.

Lord our God,
you renew us with food from heaven;
fill our hearts with the gentle love of your Spirit.
May the gifts we have received in this life
lead us to the gift of eternal joy.
We ask this through Christ our Lord.

Prayer after communion, Votive Mass for the Holy Spirit

Group Session Three

Opening Prayer

A: Happy are those whose way is blameless,
who walk in the law of the Lord.
Happy are those who keep his decrees,
who seek him with their whole heart,
who also do no wrong, but walk in his ways.

B: You have commanded your precepts to be kept diligently.
O that my ways may be steadfast
in keeping your statutes!
Then I shall not be put to shame,
having my eyes fixed on all your commandments.

A: I will praise you with an upright heart,
when I learn your righteous ordinances.
I will observe your statutes;
do not utterly forsake me.

B: How can young people keep their way pure?
By guarding it according to your word.
With my whole heart I seek you;
do not let me stray from your commandments.

All: Glory be…

From Psalm 118 (119)

Come, Holy Spirit, fill the hearts of your faithful
and kindle in them the fire of your love.
Send forth your spirit and they shall be created
and you will renew the face of the earth.

See Psalm 103:30 and Gospel Acclamation for Pentecost

Let us listen carefully to the Word of the Lord,
and attend to it with the ear of our hearts.
Let us welcome it, and faithfully put it into practice.

St. Benedict of Nursia (c.480-c.547) adapted

Explore the Scriptures John 16:1-11

'I have said these things to you to keep you from stumbling. They will put you out of the synagogues. Indeed, an hour is coming when those who kill you will think that by doing so they are offering worship to God. And they will do this because they have not known the Father or me. But I have said these things to you so that when their hour comes you may remember that I told you about them.

'I did not say these things to you from the beginning, because I was with you. But now I am going to him who sent me; yet none of you asks me, "Where are you going?" But because I have said these things to you, sorrow has filled your hearts. Nevertheless, I tell you the truth: it is to your advantage that I go away, for if I do not go away, the Advocate will not come to you; but if I go, I will send him to you. And when he comes, he will prove the world wrong about sin and righteousness and judgement: about sin, because they do not believe in me; about righteousness, because I am going to the Father and you will see me no longer; about judgement, because the ruler of this world has been condemned.

Before the passage is read again with a different voice you may wish to share a word, an image or a phrase that has struck you. These thoughts can be discussed further after the second reading.

Reflection

It can be easy to dismiss the Commandments as archaic rules and the matter of sin as having little relevance in our own lives After all, we are not murderers! So, it follows that there would be no need for an examination of conscience and Christ's death on the Cross would be rather superfluous. This line of thinking may seem somewhat startling. Yet, at his last supper with his apostles, Christ himself insisted that his leaving was for our benefit – our salvation – and that only through his dying would he be able to send us the Advocate who will convince or, as the above translation has phrased it, prove the world wrong about sin.

Christ himself encountered loneliness and the widespread rejection of his mission during his own lifetime. By his own death on the Cross, he ensured that we would not face life's challenges alone and unaided. At baptism, Christ poured the love of God into our hearts (Romans 5:5). Anointed, he lovingly infused His Spirit in each of us to be our guide. There, in our hearts, deep in the core of our very beings, the Holy Spirit imprints Christ's own understanding of the Decalogue – teaching us how to love God and our neighbour.

In his encyclical, *Veritatis Splendor*, Pope John Paul II affirmed that 'in the depth of his conscience man detects a law which he does not impose on himself, but which holds him to obedience. Always summoning him to love good and avoid evil…' (VS, 54). Just as St. Paul in his letters cautioned the Romans to set aside worldly desires, Pope John Paul II reminds us not to simply conform our minds to the secular values of this world but to be transformed by the workings of the Holy Spirit who is there to help us contemplate the mystery of sin lingering in the chaos of our world (VS, 62). In the depths of our hearts, the Holy Spirit takes us to a deeper level of understanding, bringing us to the truth so that we can evaluate our own lives and deeds in light of this higher order. In doing so, the Holy Spirit convinces us of our sinfulness and leads us to seek forgiveness. Through his efforts, we grow in holiness ever closer to Christ who so lovingly offered himself on the Cross for our sins and rose again to give each of us the offer of eternal salvation – to life everlasting in his embrace.

In what concrete ways can we demonstrate our love for Jesus Christ who so lovingly offered himself on the Cross for our sins? How can we demonstrate our joy for the gift of the Holy Spirit who works to reconcile us with God the Father?

Leader: Aloud or in the silence of our hearts let us bring to the Father our thanks (pause)…

Leader: In sorrow let us ask the Father for forgiveness (pause)…

Leader: With confidence let us entrust to the Father our cares and concerns (pause)…

Closing Prayer

Heavenly King,
Consoler Spirit,
Spirit of Truth,
present everywhere and filling all things,
treasure of all good and Source of all life,
come dwell in us,
cleanse and save us,
You who are All Good!

Byzantine Liturgy, Pentecost Vespers, Troparion

Today's Second Reading *I Corinthians 1:22-25 (NRSV translation)*

For Jews demand signs and Greeks desire wisdom, but we proclaim Christ crucified, a stumbling-block to Jews and foolishness to Gentiles, but to those who are the called, both Jews and Greeks, Christ the power of God and the wisdom of God. For God's foolishness is wiser than human wisdom, and God's weakness is stronger than human strength.

Who is Jesus for us? Does his death make sense to us? Pray that the Holy Spirit grants us the gifts of wisdom and understanding to realise the truth which Christ's life and death reveal, and that we may know God's will for us.

Breathe in me, O Holy Spirit,
that my thoughts may all be holy.
Act in me, O Holy Spirit,
that my work, too, may be holy.
Draw my heart, O Holy Spirit,
that I love but what is holy.
Strengthen me, O Holy Spirit,
to defend all that is holy.
Guard me, then, O Holy Spirit,
that I always may be holy.
Amen.

St. Augustine (354-430)

Dying and rising with Christ

So it is with the resurrection of the dead. What is sown is perishable, what is raised is imperishable. It is sown in dishonour, it is raised in glory. It is sown in weakness, it is raised in power. It is sown a physical body, it is raised a spiritual body. If there is a physical body, there is also a spiritual body. Thus it is written, 'The first man, Adam, became a living being'; the last Adam became a life-giving spirit.

I Corinthians 15:42-45

In his letters, St. Paul proclaimed that our Father joyfully responded to Christ's act of love, the gift of himself, with the resurrection – enthroning Christ at his right hand and enabling Christ to send us his Spirit not just to be with certain individuals from time to time as was the case with the prophets and other Old Testament figures but in all for all time. In other words, Christ's sending of the Holy Spirit is ongoing. At our baptism, Christ lovingly infuses each of us with the gift of the Holy Spirit and invites us to join him in his divinity – to die with him and rise to a new life. Through the sacraments and the use of sacramental signs, Christ draws each of us to himself. While the relatively recent tsunami underscores water's potential for death and destruction and its life giving qualities are well known, baptismal water leads us beyond the visible to contemplate the invisible - to die with Christ, to rise to a new life in him and to receive his Spirit, to have the love of God poured into our hearts.

Come down, O love divine,
Seek thou this soul of mine,
and visit it with thine own ardour glowing;
O Comforter draw near,
within my heart appear,
and kindle it, thy holy flame bestowing.

Bianco da Siena (c.1350 - 1434)

Temple of the Holy Spirit

But you are not in the flesh; you are in the Spirit, since the Spirit of God dwells in you.

Romans 8:9

Starting out in the working world, we often think of ourselves as being 'on the bottom rung of the ladder' with the prospect of years of hard work to earn our place nearer the top. In baptism, however, we are gratuitously given our greatest honour – we are made a child of God and given new life in Christ. The Holy Spirit is infused in us and marks us with 'the seal of the Lord', an indelible mark of our belonging to Christ (CCC, 1272). Through the workings of the Holy Spirit, this divine life in Christ is freely given to each of us along with the task of sharing in Christ's mission. Often termed, our 'call to holiness', we are asked to build up our life in Christ – to imitate him in our daily living.

This task – our personal response to this wondrous gift of his love - may sometimes seem rather daunting but Christ has not left us to our own devices. Through the indwelling of His Spirit, we are not alone. The Holy Spirit is there to help us share in Christ's mission in this world. Through the visible work of the Church, the celebration of the sacraments, we are continually supported and nourished for this endeavour. Just as the apostles received a special power at Pentecost, through the sacrament of Confirmation, we too are given a special strengthening to confront earthly temptations and to help us to proclaim our faith. Thus, derived from early Church tradition, the liturgical gestures – the laying on of hands and the anointing with the oil of chrism – are used to point to the transcendent, our life in the Spirit. Through the sacrament we are strengthened to live as Christians, to be Christ-like in this world (CCC, 1289 and 1303).

O Lord our God,
help us to realise our dependence on one another
each dispensing and receiving the graces and gifts you bestow
remembering that, unless we do this for love of You, it is worth nothing.
Amen.

Adapted from the Dialogue of Saint Catherine of Siena (1347-1380)

Predisposition

Now we have received not the spirit of the world but the Spirit that is from God, so that we may understand the gifts bestowed on us by God.

1 Corinthians 2:12

Gifts can be received with great excitement and give years of great pleasure/memories or they can be quickly stored away without ever being unwrapped. Baptisms are often accompanied with great celebrations, but sadly, these spiritual gifts are often left unopened, their meaning long forgotten. In his homily at World Youth Day 2008, Pope Benedict invites us to contemplate our response to the wondrous gift that we receive at baptism:

'Yet this power, the grace of the Spirit, is not something we can merit or achieve, but only receive as pure gift. God's love can only unleash its power when it is allowed to change us from within. We have to let it break through the hard crust of our indifference, our spiritual weariness, our blind conformity to the spirit of this age. Only then can we let it ignite our imagination and shape our deepest desires.'

Lord Christ,
you have no body on earth but ours,
no hands but ours, no feet but ours.
Ours are the eyes through which your compassion
must look out on the world.
Ours are the feet by which you may still
go about doing good.
Ours are the hands with which you bless people now.
Bless our minds and bodies, that we may be a blessing to others.
Amen.

St. Theresa of Avila (1515-1582)

The Spirit's help

Likewise the Spirit helps us in our weakness; for we do not know how to pray as we ought, but that very Spirit intercedes with sighs too deep for words.

Romans 8:26

The word 'seal' might initially call to mind a corporate imprint denoting authenticity or some legalistic authority. While the Holy Spirit does bring us to the truth, we are not enslaved! On the contrary, by becoming adopted children of the Father at baptism, we are receiving a gift without contractual obligations – perhaps more akin to a standing invitation awaiting our response. Permanently infused in our hearts, the Holy Spirit is with us always – offering to help us to respond to this wondrous gift of our Father's love. However, with so many distractions, the invitation can be overlooked or the response be almost perfunctory. On our own, our prayers can sometimes become a litany of personal desires or simply a stream of empty words. Yet, we are not alone for, dwelling in our hearts, the Holy Spirit is there to guide from within, to stir us from the depths of our innermost being so as to fix our gaze on the risen Christ.

Lord Jesus Christ,
take all my freedom,
my memory, my understanding, and my will.
All that I have and cherish
you have given me.
I surrender it all to be guided by your will.
Your grace and your love
are wealth enough for me.
Give me these, Lord Jesus,
and I ask for nothing more.

St. Ignatius Loyola (c. 1491-1556)

When he had said this, he breathed on them and said to them, 'Receive the Holy Spirit. If you forgive the sins of any, they are forgiven them; if you retain the sins of any, they are retained.'

John 20: 22-24

In this week's group reflection, we contemplated how the Holy Spirit convinces us of sin. In the depths of our hearts, the Holy Spirit takes us to a deeper level of understanding, bringing us to the truth so that we can evaluate our own lives and deeds in light of this higher order. In doing so, the Holy Spirit convinces us of our sinfulness. Just as Christ came to save us, the Holy Spirit, too, does not want to leave us to languish in a disordered world – where, sadly, we have freely chosen to unseat God in favour of our own self-interests. As our Counselor, the Holy Spirit is there to stir our conscience, to prompt us to seek forgiveness for our shortcomings. While acknowledging that it is not easy to control our worldly desires and that resolving to turn one's back on sin demands great effort, Pope John Paul II reminds us that it is by our sacrifices that we are united with Christ who lovingly suffered on the Cross for our salvation (*Dominum et vivificantem*, 44-45).

The Lord bless you and keep you.
May He show His face to you and have mercy.
May He turn His countenance to you and give you peace.
The Lord bless you!

The Blessing of St. Francis of Assisi to Brother Leo (see also Numbers 6: 24-26)

Tomorrow's Second Reading *Ephesians 2:4-10 (NRSV translation)*

But God, who is rich in mercy, out of the great love with which he loved us even when we were dead through our trespasses, made us alive together with Christ – by grace you have been saved – and raised us up with him and seated us with him in the heavenly places in Christ Jesus, so that in the ages to come he might show the immeasurable riches of his grace in kindness towards us in Christ Jesus. For by grace you have been saved through faith, and this is not your own doing; it is the gift of God – not the result of works, so that no one may boast. For we are what he has made us, created in Christ Jesus for good works, which God prepared beforehand to be our way of life.

The theme permeating the readings today is one of grace and forgiveness. In the first reading where the Israelites had broken the covenant (2 Chronicles 36:14-23), God stayed his hand sending messenger after messenger until 'there was no further remedy'. He then provided an instrument of redemption in Cyrus the king of Persia. In his letter to the Ephesians, written to exhort believers to a standard of behaviour in keeping with their status as children of the light, Paul calls the Ephesians and all members of the Church to strive in response to God's greatest gift, Christ Jesus, our redeemer.

Lord our God,
you renew us with food from heaven;
fill our hearts with the gentle love of your Spirit.
May the gifts we have received in this life ,
lead us to the gift of eternal joy.
We ask this through Christ our Lord.

Prayer after communion, Votive Mass for the Holy Spirit

Group Session Four

Opening Prayer

A:	Glorious are you, more majestic than the everlasting mountains. At your rebuke, O God of Jacob, both rider and horse lay stunned. But you indeed are awesome! Who can stand before you when once your anger is roused?
B:	From the heavens you uttered judgement; the earth feared and was still when God rose up to establish judgement, to save all the oppressed of the earth.
A:	Make vows to the Lord your God, and perform them; let all who are around him bring gifts to the one who is awesome, who cuts off the spirit of princes, who inspires fear in the kings of the earth.
All:	Glory be…

From Psalm 75 (76)

Come, Holy Spirit, fill the hearts of your faithful
and kindle in them the fire of your love.
Send forth your spirit and they shall be created
and you will renew the face of the earth.

See Psalm 103:30 and Gospel Acclamation for Pentecost

Let us listen carefully to the Word of the Lord,
and attend to it with the ear of our hearts.
Let us welcome it, and faithfully put it into practice.

St. Benedict of Nursia (c.480-c.547) adapted

Explore the Scriptures *I Corinthians 12:1-11*

Now concerning spiritual gifts, brothers and sisters, I do not want you to be uninformed. You know that when you were pagans, you were enticed and led astray to idols that could not speak. Therefore I want you to understand that no one speaking by the Spirit of God ever says 'Let Jesus be cursed!' and no one can say 'Jesus is Lord' except by the Holy Spirit.

Now there are varieties of gifts, but the same Spirit; and there are varieties of services, but to the same Lord; and there are varieties of activities, but it is the same God who activates all of them in everyone. To each is given the manifestation of the Spirit for the common good. To one is given through the Spirit the utterance of wisdom, and to another the utterance of knowledge according to the same Spirit, to another faith by the same Spirit, to another gifts of healing by the one Spirit, to another the working of miracles, to another prophecy, to another the discernment of spirits, to another various kinds of tongues, to another the interpretation of tongues. All these are activated by one and the same Spirit, who allots to each one individually just as the Spirit chooses.

Before the passage is read again with a different voice you may wish to share a word, an image or a phrase that has struck you. These thoughts can be discussed further after the second reading.

Reflection

It is possible to reflect on our lives in terms of achievements accomplished or milestones reached; qualifications gained, promotions given, possessions had, birthdays celebrated. And that done, to see all of this as the work of our own hands – something to do with us individually, before it has anything to do with others, let alone God. In this passage St Paul reminds us that what we have achieved, and above all the faith we have, is first and foremost the gift of the Holy Spirit. 'No one' he says, 'can say "Jesus is Lord" except by the Holy Spirit.'

Attributing everything we accomplish to the working of the Holy Spirit is rather humbling. What credit have we a right to take? Yet, if this is true for 'me' it is true for everyone. If I cannot claim credit for what I have done, neither can anyone else for what they have done. Here, if you like, there is no room for pride or elitism, just that simple recognition that everything we receive is gift. Again, where others have been gifted in a way we would have liked, it's easy to see them as having all the luck. Yet here too, St Paul is very clear. Whatever gifts we have, and whatever gifts others may have, none of us have been gifted for personal gratification. On the contrary, all have received so as to work towards the common good.

To what extent do you see the gifts you have received as being gifts for you – your well-being, your happiness – as opposed to gifts for others, including the stranger? What limits can we fairly set to our giving?

Leader: Aloud or in the silence of our hearts let us bring to the Father our thanks (pause)…

Leader: In sorrow let us ask the Father for forgiveness (pause)…

Leader: With confidence let us entrust to the Father our cares and concerns (pause)…

Closing Prayer

Heavenly King,
Consoler Spirit,
Spirit of Truth,
present everywhere and filling all things,
treasure of all good and Source of all life,
come dwell in us,
cleanse and save us,
You who are All Good!

Byzantine Liturgy, Pentecost Vespers, Troparion

Today's Second Reading *Ephesians 2:4-10 (NRSV translation)*

But God, who is rich in mercy, out of the great love with which he loved us even when we were dead through our trespasses, made us alive together with Christ – by grace you have been saved – and raised us up with him and seated us with him in the heavenly places in Christ Jesus, so that in the ages to come he might show the immeasurable riches of his grace in kindness towards us in Christ Jesus. For by grace you have been saved through faith, and this is not your own doing; it is the gift of God – not the result of works, so that no one may boast. For we are what he has made us, created in Christ Jesus for good works, which God prepared beforehand to be our way of life.

Another translation of this passage talks of you as 'God's work of art' and Isaiah wrote that 'we are the clay, the work of God's hand' (Isaiah 64:8). What, if anything, is preventing you from seeing yourself as 'God's work of art'? What steps can you take this Lent to change this and realise that, by God's grace, we have been raised up in Christ Jesus?

Breathe in me, O Holy Spirit,
that my thoughts may all be holy.
Act in me, O Holy Spirit,
that my work, too, may be holy.
Draw my heart, O Holy Spirit,
that I love but what is holy.
Strengthen me, O Holy Spirit,
to defend all that is holy.
Guard me, then, O Holy Spirit,
that I always may be holy.
Amen.

St. Augustine (354-430)

Knowing the Spirit

This is the Spirit of truth, whom the world cannot receive, because it neither sees him nor knows him…he will not speak on his own, but will speak whatever he hears

John 14:17, 16:13

Pointing to these verses from St. John's Gospel the Catechism speaks of the Holy Spirit's 'self-effacement'. It is not the Spirit's voice that the Spirit wishes to be heard, but the voice of Christ, the Word. Indeed, it is only in his working to reveal Christ, and to predispose us to welcoming Christ, that we come to know the Holy Spirit (CCC, 687).

The Catechism goes on to say that the Church is the place where we know the Holy Spirit. As well as to the Scriptures, Tradition and the Church's Magisterium (Teaching Authority), the Catechism points us to the Sacraments, to prayer, and to the lives, witness and ministry of the saints and others, where the Holy Spirit can be found at work, putting us into communion with Christ (CCC, 688). In this fourth week of reflection on the Holy Spirit we will look at four New Testament figures and ask how the Holy Spirit can be seen at work in their lives.

God, our Father,
you inspired speech in different tongues
to proclaim one faith.
We pray that you may strengthen our faith
and fulfil our hope of seeing you face to face.
Amen.

Roman Missal, Solemn Blessing, Holy Spirit, adapted

Simeon, a righteous and devout man

'Now there was a man in Jerusalem whose name was Simeon; this man was righteous and devout, looking forward to the consolation of Israel, and the Holy Spirit rested on him. It had been revealed to him by the Holy Spirit that he would not see death before he had seen the Lord's Messiah. Guided by the Spirit, Simeon came into the temple; and when the parents brought in the child Jesus, to do for him what was customary under the law, Simeon took him in his arms and praised God'.

Luke 2: 25 - 28

We are told in the Scriptures that Simeon went to the temple at the prompting of the Holy Spirit and that, before this, the Holy Spirit had promised he would see the Messiah before he died. What must the Holy Spirit's promise have meant to Simeon? What purpose did it give him? How did it shape his life, his thoughts, his actions? Much as that childhood longing for Christmas, that excited expectation, consumed our thoughts, even governed our actions, so the Spirit worked in Simeon, a 'righteous and devout' man.

At last, all-powerful Master,
you give leave to your servant
to go in peace, according to your promise.
For my eyes have seen your salvation,
which you have prepared for all nations,
the light to enlighten the Gentiles,
and give glory to Israel, your people.
Amen.

Nunc Dimittis (or Song of Simeon) Luke 2:29-32

Mary, the favoured one

'Greetings, favoured one! The Lord is with you…Do not be afraid…for you have found favour with God...The angel said to her, 'The Holy Spirit will come upon you, and the power of the Most High will overshadow you; therefore the child to be born will be holy; he will be called Son of God'.

Luke 1:28, 30, 35

These words, addressed to Mary by the angel Gabriel, speak of someone who had been singled out or specially favoured by God. Mary recognised this for herself. 'The Mighty One has done great things for me' (Luke 1:49). However, the Holy Spirit that overshadowed Mary at the moment of Christ's Incarnation – his becoming man in Mary's womb – had already been at work in Mary's life, ensuring that she was conceived without the stain of original sin and capable, as the Catechism puts it, of 'welcoming the inexpressible gift of the Almighty' (CCC, 722).

From the Catechism

721. For the first time in the plan of salvation and because his Spirit had prepared her, the Father found the *dwelling-place* where his Son and his Spirit could dwell among men.

My soul glorifies the Lord, my spirit rejoices in God, my Saviour.
He looks on his servant in her lowliness;
henceforth all ages will call me blessed.
The Almighty works marvels for me. Holy his name!
His mercy is from age to age, on those who fear him.
He puts forth his arm in strength and scatters the proud-hearted.
He casts the mighty from their thrones and raises the lowly.
He fills the starving with good things, sends the rich away empty.
He protects Israel, his servant, remembering his mercy,
the mercy promised to our fathers,
to Abraham and his sons for ever.

Magnificat (or Song of Mary) Luke 1:46-55

The Samaritan Woman at the Well

Jesus answered her, 'If you knew the gift of God, and who it is that is saying to you, "give me a drink," you would have asked him, and he would have given you living water.' 'Sir, you have no bucket, and the well is deep. Where do you get that living water?...' Jesus said to her, 'Everyone who drinks of this water will be thirsty again, but those who drink of the water I will give them will never be thirsty. The water that I will give will become in them a spring of water gushing up to eternal life.' The woman said to him, 'Sir, give me this water, so that I may never be thirsty or have to keep coming here to draw water.'

John 4:10-11, 13-15

The 'living water' Christ speaks of in this exchange with the Samaritan Woman is the Holy Spirit. As John points out later on in his Gospel, Christ uses 'living water' as a metaphor for the Holy Spirit, inviting those who believe in him to come to him and drink (John 7:38-39). Even though the outpouring of the Holy Spirit at Pentecost was yet to take place we can see from John's account of the Samaritan Woman that the well which would spring up to eternal life was at work in her. For sure she has not fully understood, for she supposes that this water would prevent physical thirst, but there is a request, a desire, for what Christ promises. 'Sir' she says, 'give me this water'. Indeed, it was on the basis of her testimony that many came to believe in Christ (John 4:39).

Father, all-powerful and ever-living God,
when your Son asked the woman of Samaria for water to drink,
he had already prepared for her the gift of faith.
In his thirst to receive her faith
he awakened in her heart the fire of your love.
Grant that we too may keep the fire of faith burning in our hearts.
Amen.

Roman Missal, Preface for the Third Sunday of Lent, adapted

St. Paul

So Ananias went and entered the house. He laid his hands on Saul and said, 'Brother Saul, the Lord Jesus, who appeared to you on your way here, has sent me so that you may regain your sight and be filled with the Holy Spirit.' And immediately something like scales fell from his eyes, and his sight was restored. Then he got up and was baptised, and after taking some food, he regained his strength.

Acts 9:17-19

Acts makes it clear that the coming of the Holy Spirit had an immediate impact on Paul's life. Astounding the Jewish Community, and those who knew of his previous antipathy towards believers, Paul began to proclaim Jesus as the Son of God (Acts 9:20-22). Time and again Paul draws our attention to the power of the Spirit. It is the Spirit that has enabled him to accomplish all that he has accomplished (Romans 15:17-19). In 1 Corinthians (2:3-4) he speaks of going to them in 'weakness, fear and trembling' and convincing them with 'a demonstration of the Spirit and of power'. In Galatians (3:1-5) he reprimands those who seem to have forgotten that it is an attentiveness to the Spirit – to believing what they have heard – not 'doing the works of the law' that has seen the working of miracles. Indeed it is through the Holy Spirit that God's love is poured into our hearts (Romans 5:5) and that our mortal bodies will be raised to life (Romans 8:11).

Hear our prayer Lord Jesus,
that we may follow the example of St. Paul,
who tells us to avoid dissipation
and to be filled with the Spirit.
We pray for the strength and joy
to give thanks, always and everywhere,
through you to God, our Father.
Amen.

Adapted from Ephesians 5:18-20

Tomorrow's Second Reading *Hebrews 5:7-9 (NRSV translation)*

In the days of his flesh, Jesus offered up prayers and supplications, with loud cries and tears, to the one who was able to save him from death, and he was heard because of his reverent submission. Although he was a Son, he learned obedience through what he suffered; and having been made perfect, he became the source of eternal salvation for all who obey him.

The identity of the author of the letter to the Hebrews is unknown to all but God but the letter contains some similarities to the Pauline correspondence. It addresses the redemptive power of Jesus Christ who, knowing full well what was coming, responded with resolute obedience. This reading is part of a longer passage which describes Jesus' priestly characteristics; Jesus who was both high priest of the new covenant and the Lamb who takes away our sin. The author of Hebrews exhorts listeners to follow Christ as a model and to take personal and concrete steps to meld their will to that of the Father.

Lord our God,
you renew us with food from heaven;
fill our hearts with the gentle love of your Spirit.
May the gifts we have received in this life
lead us to the gift of eternal joy.
We ask this through Christ our Lord
Amen.

Prayer after communion, Votive Mass for the Holy Spirit

Group Session Five

Opening Prayer

A: Give us, O God, your spirit of wisdom

B: Give us, O God, your spirit of understanding

A: Give us, O God, your spirit of fortitude

B: Give us, O God, your spirit of counsel

A: Give us, O God, your spirit of wisdom

B: Give us, O God, true knowledge

A: Give us, O God, a sense of your presence and greatness

B: Blessed, O God, are your children who hope in you

see Isaiah 11:2-3

Come, Holy Spirit, fill the hearts of your faithful
and kindle in them the fire of your love.
Send forth your spirit and they shall be created
and you will renew the face of the earth.

See Psalm 103:30 and Gospel Acclamation for Pentecost

Let us listen carefully to the Word of the Lord,
and attend to it with the ear of our hearts.
Let us welcome it, and faithfully put it into practice.

St. Benedict of Nursia (c.480-c.547) adapted

Explore the Scriptures Isaiah 11:1-9

A shoot shall come out from the stock of Jesse, and a branch shall grow out of his roots. The spirit of the Lord shall rest on him, the spirit of wisdom and understanding, the spirit of counsel and might, the spirit of knowledge and the fear of the Lord. His delight shall be in the fear of the Lord.

He shall not judge by what his eyes see, or decide by what his ears hear; but with righteousness he shall judge the poor, and decide with equity for the meek of the earth; he shall strike the earth with the rod of his mouth, and with the breath of his lips he shall kill the wicked. Righteousness shall be the belt around his waist, and faithfulness the belt around his loins.

The wolf shall live with the lamb, the leopard shall lie down with the kid, the calf and the lion and the fatling together, and a little child shall lead them. The cow and the bear shall graze, their young shall lie down together; and the lion shall eat straw like the ox. The nursing child shall play over the hole of the asp, and the weaned child shall put its hand on the adder's den. They will not hurt or destroy on all my holy mountain; for the earth will be full of the knowledge of the Lord as the waters cover the sea.

Before the passage is read again with a different voice you may wish to share a word, an image or a phrase that has struck you. These thoughts can be discussed further after the second reading.

Reflection

We can find it difficult to live with disorder. Making sense out of chaos is a plain desire for most. Millions and millions of years ago the Holy Spirit did precisely this, when the world was a formless void and darkness covered the face of the deep. The power of the Holy Spirit, creating and transforming the world, can change people too – we'd be foolish to think otherwise.

If we truly believe in the transforming power of the Holy Spirit, in a generous God, who has and will give us all that attains to holiness, then the challenge of living out the call to holiness is something we can approach in hope and trust. In God, in Christ, in the power of the Holy Spirit, everything is possible. In the Apostolic Exhortation, *Sacramentum Caritatis* (Sacrament of Love), Pope Benedict calls us to a greater appreciation of the transforming power of God's Holy Spirit, reminding us that it is through the outpouring of the Holy Spirit – 'Christ's first gift to those who believe'

– that the apostles were able to undertake their mission and that Christ 'continues to be present and active in his Church, starting with her vital centre which is the Eucharist' (SC, 12).

The worldview described in the passage from Isaiah is quite the opposite of the world in which we live today. This 'alien' world is an image of the kingdom, a world utterly transformed by Christ, the 'shoot that comes from the stock of Jesse'. In Christ was the fullness of the Holy Spirit, he had the spiritual gifts in abundance. We believe that the seven gifts of the Holy Spirit are given to help us 'complete and perfect the virtues' we have already as we wait for the revealing of our Lord Jesus Christ (1 Corinthians 1:6-7). By living out these gifts we can help the Lord to bring about a radical transformation in our lives and the communities in which we live. By living out these gifts we will be witnessing to the kingdom prophesied by Isaiah and which we long to see.

Where have I allowed the chaos of the world to blind me from my duty and privilege of sharing in Christ's mission? How might I open myself to God's generosity and demonstrate my acceptance of this love to the world at large? In this way, how might I be able to affect change in the wider world?

From Redemptoris Missio

92. Like the apostles after Christ's Ascension, the Church must gather in the Upper Room 'together with Mary, the Mother of Jesus' (Acts 1:14), in order to pray for the Spirit and to gain strength and courage to carry out the missionary mandate. We too, like the apostles, need to be transformed and guided by the Spirit.

Leader: Aloud or in the silence of our hearts let us bring to the Father our thanks (pause)…

Leader: In sorrow let us ask the Father for forgiveness (pause)…

Leader: With confidence let us entrust to the Father our cares and concerns (pause)…

Closing Prayer

Heavenly King,
Consoler Spirit,
Spirit of Truth,
present everywhere and filling all things,
treasure of all good and Source of all life,
come dwell in us,
cleanse and save us,
You who are All Good!

Byzantine Liturgy, Pentecost Vespers, Troparion

Today's Second Reading *Hebrews 5:7-9 (NRSV translation)*

In the days of his flesh, Jesus offered up prayers and supplications, with loud cries and tears, to the one who was able to save him from death, and he was heard because of his reverent submission. Although he was a Son, he learned obedience through what he suffered; and having been made perfect, he became the source of eternal salvation for all who obey him.

Christ was utterly obedient to the will of his Father, even to accepting death. He called out but learnt to submit to his Father's will and we are asked to do the same, indeed, we pray for this each time we say the 'Our Father'. Where have we called out 'with loud cries and tears' but still not learnt to welcome God's will for us?

Breathe in me, O Holy Spirit,
that my thoughts may all be holy.
Act in me, O Holy Spirit,
that my work, too, may be holy.
Draw my heart, O Holy Spirit,
that I love but what is holy.
Strengthen me, O Holy Spirit,
to defend all that is holy.
Guard me, then, O Holy Spirit,
that I always may be holy.
Amen.

St. Augustine (354-430)

Right Judgement and Wisdom

'Give your servant therefore an understanding mind to govern your people, able to discern between "good and evil..." God said to him, 'because you have asked this, and have not asked for yourself long life or riches, or for the life of your enemies, but have asked for yourself understanding to discern what is right, I now do according to your word.'

1 Kings 3:9, 11-12

Isn't life complicated? We try to keep things simple but there are so many things to keep simple and they're all interconnected anyway. Solomon asked the Lord for the gift of wisdom, an understanding mind that could discern right and wrong. This is the type of clarity that we so often thirst for. We have been gifted with a desire for the things of God, a desire to direct our lives towards him and the gift to warn us when we stray from this path. Such clarity as was given to Solomon is given to us by the Spirit.

Reflecting on my life decisions, what part has prayer and invocation of the Holy Spirit played? What choices do I face at the moment? How might this reflection on the Holy Spirit change the way I make decisions?

From the Catechism

1831. The seven gifts of the Holy Spirit are wisdom, understanding, counsel, fortitude, knowledge, piety and fear of the Lord. They belong in their fullness to Christ, Son of David. They complete and perfect the virtues of those who receive them. They make the faithful docile in readily obeying divine inspirations.

O God, send forth your Holy Spirit into my heart
that I may perceive,
into my mind that I may remember,
and into my soul that I may meditate.
Inspire me to speak with piety, holiness, tenderness and mercy.
Teach, guide and direct my thoughts and senses from beginning to end.
May your grace ever help and correct me,
and may I be strengthened now with wisdom from on high,
for the sake of your infinite mercy.
Amen.

St. Anthony of Padua (1195-1231)

Knowledge

All the words of my mouth are righteous; there is nothing twisted or crooked in them. They are all straight to one who understands and right to those who find knowledge. Take my instruction instead of silver, and knowledge rather than choice gold; for wisdom is better than jewels, and all that you may desire cannot compare with her.

Proverbs 8:8-11

We are called to know God, to love him and serve him. We are made to praise God with the very core of our being. Our worship of Our Father is not to be a half-hearted affair, it is for our minds as well as our hearts. Worship is not just about getting caught up with our sins, telling him how good he is, how you are going to live for him but telling him that you know he exists, that he sent Jesus so that we can comprehend him a little.

God is a God who loves us so much that he reveals himself to us. First to the prophets, then in his Word, Jesus Christ, God made man. The Holy Spirit is sent to bear witness to this truth and to help us to do the same.

Absolute and all knowing God,
nothing is hidden from your sight.
Since the beginning, all knowledge existed within you.
Make me aware of what is meant to be,
permit my soul to understand it,
and wisdom to agree with its outcome.
Amen.

Understanding

'When anyone hears the word of the kingdom and does not understand it, the evil one comes and snatches away what is "sown in the heart..." But the one who hears the word and understands it bears fruit and yields in one case a hundredfold, in another sixty, and in another thirty.'

Matthew 13:19, 23

The Holy Spirit, Pope John Paul II wrote, helps people 'to understand the correct meaning of the content of Christ's message… in the midst of changing conditions and circumstances' (*Dominium et vivificantem*, 4). In an increasingly secular world, in the midst of these changing circumstances we are called to bear witness to the word of the kingdom and to bear fruit. Following the right path is often not easy and so we pray to the Spirit that we receive his gift of understanding – the 'avoidance of evil' (Job 28:28). Understanding is not solely about knowing how to act in any given situation or just being a good person but in acknowledging the source of all of our efforts and goodness… Jesus Christ, whom the Spirit reveals.

Lord Jesus Christ,
help us to grow in understanding
to attain through the gifts of your Spirit maturity as Christians
and so to witness more fully to your goodness.
Amen.

Reverence and Fear of the Lord

Therefore, since we are receiving a kingdom that cannot be shaken, let us give thanks, by which we offer to God an acceptable worship with reverence and awe; for indeed our God is a consuming fire.

Hebrews 12:28-29

There is a term for an abnormal fear of divine punishment - Theophobia. This is not what we are to understand by Fear of the Lord. When we are too scared to do something we are prevented from loving. Fear of being punished, servile fear, can paralyse us. Yet, we readily acknowledge our God as Father and John writes that 'God is Love' (1 John 4:8). Fear of the Lord is not a fear of retribution from a vengeful deity but fear that each day we may place barriers, large or small, between us and his love shown to us in Jesus Christ. Staying focused on God's love, through prayer and actions, will 'gladden the heart', we who try to stay in the love of the Lord will be 'blessed at the last' (Ecclesiasticus 1:11-25).

All powerful and ever-living God,
how wonderful the work of your hands,
how awesome your ways.
Grant us your Spirit that we may see
your beauty in those around us and
keep us true to your love which gladdens the humblest heart.
Amen.

Friday of Week Five

Courage

I hereby command you: be strong and courageous; do not be frightened or dismayed, for the Lord your God is with you wherever you go.

Joshua 1:9

This short passage from Joshua echoes Jesus' promise to his disciples and to us (Matthew 28:20). Telling us not to be afraid and reminding us of his presence appears to be a favourite theme of God. 'Be not afraid' the angel said to Mary and Joseph when announcing the coming of the child Emmanuel, God with us (Luke 1:30 and Matthew 1:20). Jesus himself told his followers to have no fear many times (e.g. Matthew 10:31, 14:27, 17:7, 28:10). No matter how often we feel as though we are struggling alone, we can take solace in the Spirit's presence in our lives – the Holy Spirit who gifts us the 'strength, peace and courage to overcome difficulties' (CCC, 1520). Likewise we can find help in the examples of Mary and Joseph who took God at his word and gave themselves over to his will in all things.

I pray for the strength and courage
to be truly obedient to Jesus,
even if he calls me to go where I would rather not go.

Henri J. M. Nouwen

Tomorrow's Second Reading *Philippians 2:6-11 (NRSV translation)*

Christ Jesus, though he was in the form of God, did not regard equality with God as something to be exploited, but emptied himself, taking the form of a slave, being born in human likeness. And being found in human form, he humbled himself and became obedient to the point of death – even death on a cross. Therefore God also highly exalted him and gave him the name that is above every name, so that at the name of Jesus every knee should bend, in heaven and on earth and under the earth, and every tongue should confess that Jesus Christ is Lord, to the glory of God the Father.

In the Old Testament reading today we hear about the suffering servant, humbled and insulted. The image of Jesus suffering is brought immediately to mind. This passage from St. Paul's letter to the Philippians, written from prison, invites us to follow the whole life of Christ from incarnation and birth to death and his reigning with majesty in heaven. The Church at Philippi in Macedonia is asked by Paul to find unity through unselfishness and to share the joy that suffering in union with Christ brings about.

God our Father,
complete the work you have begun
and keep the gifts of the Holy Spirit
active in the hearts of your people.
Make us ready to live his Gospel
and eager to do his will.
May we never be ashamed
to proclaim to all the world Christ crucified
living and reigning for ever and ever.
Amen.

Final blessing, Rite of Confirmation, adapted

Group Session Six

Opening Prayer

A: O most holy Trinity, Almighty God, we adore you,
who give life and vigour to every creature and
who shed light eternal where there is darkness.
We offer you our hearts, our souls and our whole being,
today and on the days to come,
that we may offer perfect praise and love to your glorious Name.

All: Amen.

B: O Father Almighty, we thank you wholeheartedly
for all the blessings and graces you have so generously given us.

All: Amen.

A: O merciful Christ Jesus,
wash away our sins with your most precious blood.
Feel the beating of our hearts and make them like your own.
Oh, dear Jesus, wipe away our tears and pardon us for our sinfulness.
Be with us, O Lord, until our dying day
that we may be worthy of your mercy and forgiveness.

All: Amen.

B: O Holy Spirit, our guide and inspiration, lead us to the right path.
And if, on our way, we encounter difficulties and trials,
do not allow us to fall or lose hope.
Grant us the graces we need daily
that we may also share our blessings.
And, when the time comes, O Holy Spirit,
lead us to the place that is secure, full of joy and eternal peace.

All: Amen.

Let us listen carefully to the Word of the Lord,
and attend to it with the ear of our hearts.
Let us welcome it, and faithfully put it into practice.

St. Benedict of Nursia (c.480-c.547) adapted

Explore the Scriptures *John 17: 1, 6-8, 11, 13, 20-23, 25-26*

After Jesus had spoken these words, he looked up to heaven and said, 'Father, the hour has come; glorify your Son so that the Son may glorify you…

I have made your name known to those whom you gave me from the world. They were yours, and you gave them to me, and they have kept your word. Now they know that everything you have given me is from you; for the words that you gave to me I have given to them, and they have received them and know in truth that I came from you; and they have believed that you sent me… And now I am no longer in the world, but they are in the world, and I am coming to you. Holy Father, protect them in your name that you have given me, so that they may be one, as we are one... Now I am coming to you, and I speak these things in the world so that they may have my joy made complete in themselves.

I ask not only on behalf of these, but also on behalf of those who will believe in me through their word, that they may all be one. As you, Father, are in me and I am in you, may they also be one in us, so that the world may believe that you have sent me. The glory that you have given me I have given them, so that they may be one, as we are one, I in them and you in me, that they may become completely one, so that the world may know that you have sent me and have loved them even as you have loved me… 'Righteous Father, the world does not know you, but I know you; and these know that you have sent me. I made your name known to them, and I will make it known, so that the love with which you have loved me may be in them, and I in them.'

Before the passage is read again with a different voice you may wish to share a word, an image or a phrase that has struck you. These thoughts can be discussed further after the second reading.

Reflection

When striving to understand what we mean by the Trinity – 'Three persons but one God' – understanding the Holy Spirit as a person, as someone with distinct characteristics, can be difficult. We can understand the Son as a person because he, quite literally, became human and walked this earth. Again, when it comes to the Father, we can understand him as a Father because we have seen his Son and heard his voice, the burning bush and Christ's baptism being examples.

In today's Scripture, taken from the final discourse before Christ's betrayal and arrest, Christ prays to the Father for the disciples who have followed him and for those of us who will come to follow him because of their preaching. Christ speaks of the love, the unity, the bond that exists between himself and the Father. It is this love or bond between the Father and the Son which is the Holy Spirit. St. Augustine helps us when he explains that what makes the Holy Spirit unique, what makes him a person, is his being that thing or quality which the Father and the Son have in common. In other words the Holy Spirit is a unifying force, not simply standing for, but 'being' communion, or as Christ expresses it in the above passage, love.

The love which Christ desires for us, the love which he prays should live in us, is the abiding presence in us of the Holy Spirit. The love which the Father and Son have for one another is the love that Christ desires to share with us. Where this love is at work in us, we are drawn into the life of God, the life of the Trinity itself.

Drawing on today's Scripture reading and reflection how would you characterise someone who is 'living in the Spirit'?

Leader: Aloud or in the silence of our hearts let us bring to the Father our thanks (pause)...

Leader: In sorrow let us ask the Father for forgiveness (pause)...

Leader: With confidence let us entrust to the Father our cares and concerns (pause)...

Closing Prayer

Heavenly King,
Consoler Spirit,
Spirit of Truth,
present everywhere and filling all things,
treasure of all good and Source of all life,
come dwell in us,
cleanse and save us,
You who are All Good!

Byzantine Liturgy, Pentecost Vespers, Troparion

Sunday of Week Six

Today's Second Reading *Philippians 2:6-11 (NRSV translation)*

Christ Jesus, though he was in the form of God, did not regard equality with God as something to be exploited, but emptied himself, taking the form of a slave, being born in human likeness. And being found in human form, he humbled himself and became obedient to the point of death – even death on a cross. Therefore God also highly exalted him and gave him the name that is above every name, so that at the name of Jesus every knee should bend, in heaven and on earth and under the earth, and every tongue should confess that Jesus Christ is Lord, to the glory of God the Father.

As we enter into Holy Week where we will call to mind the self-humbling, self-giving of Christ, let us reflect on the ways in which we put the needs of others before ourselves. Let us reflect on this lack of self-regard, self-interest, self-concern, those times and opportunities in our own lives where we unite ourselves to Christ's action on the Cross.

Breathe in me, O Holy Spirit,
that my thoughts may all be holy.
Act in me, O Holy Spirit,
that my work, too, may be holy.
Draw my heart, O Holy Spirit,
that I love but what is holy.
Strengthen me, O Holy Spirit,
to defend all that is holy.
Guard me, then, O Holy Spirit,
that I always may be holy.
Amen.

St. Augustine (354 430)

Fruits of the Spirit

The fruit of the Spirit is love, joy, peace, patience, kindness, generosity, faithfulness, gentleness, and self-control.

Galatians 5:22-23

In this particular extract from St. Paul's letter to the Galatians, Paul outlines what are called the fruits of the Holy Spirit, the qualities which should characterise a life where the Holy Spirit has been allowed to take hold – where we have been open to the gifts he offers and they are at work in our lives.

How would you characterise yourself? Which fruits of the Spirit do you think others would readily see or recognise in you?

Let nothing disturb you,
nothing scare you;
All things are passing,
God never changes!
Patient endurance
is enough;
those God possesses
will lack for nothing;
God alone suffices.

St. Theresa of Avila (1515-1582)

Tuesday of Week Six

Mission

But you will receive power when the Holy Spirit has come upon you; and you will be my witnesses in Jerusalem, in all Judea and Samaria, and to the ends of the earth.

Acts 1:8

At his baptism by John, Christ himself was anointed by the Spirit and sent on his public ministry to set the world on fire.' These words from the homily or instruction provided in the Rite of Confirmation remind us, as Christ's words in Acts do, that the Holy Spirit is given to us that we might be witnesses to the ends of the earth. As much for others, as for ourselves, the Holy Spirit lives in us. We are his instruments, empowered by him to draw others to Christ.

What example have I given to the young and recently confirmed? Have I made room for their contribution and ideas? Have I praised, encouraged and affirmed? Have I helped them to be witnesses and evangelists?

Come, Holy Spirit, fill the hearts of your faithful
and kindle in them the fire of your love.
Send forth your spirit and they shall be created
and you will renew the face of the earth.

See Psalm 103:30 and Gospel Acclamation for Pentecost

The Holy Spirit at work

They went to a place called Gethsemane; and he said to his disciples, 'Sit here while I pray.'… And going a little farther, he threw himself on the ground and prayed that, if it were possible, the hour might pass from him. He said, 'Abba, Father, for you all things are possible; remove this cup from me; yet, not what I want, but what you want.'

Mark 14:32, 35-36

'Not what I want', says Jesus, 'but what you want.' In these few words Jesus restates his love for the Father, his desire to be at one with him. It is tempting to present Christ's prayer in Gethsemane as a dialogue between these two; as if the Holy Spirit were a kind of postscript coming after the drama, the paschal mystery, that was about to unfold While St. Augustine spoke of the Holy Spirit as the bond or love between the Father and the Son we can see that here, where love is at work, the Holy Spirit is altogether present and active.

How conscious am I of the Holy Spirit's being at work in my life and relationships? How conscious am I of his being at the root of every loving thing I have done?

From Dominum et vivificantem

40. In the sacrifice of the Son of Man the Holy Spirit is present and active just as he acted in Jesus' conception, in his coming into the world, in his hidden life and in his public ministry.

Christ, innocent though you were,
you died once for our sins,
you died for the guilty, to lead us to God.
In the body you were put to death,
in the spirit you were raised to life.
For this we give thanks.

Adapted from the Responsory to the 1st reading, Easter Octave: Friday, Divine Office

Holy Thursday

After he had washed their feet, had put on his robe and had returned to the table, he said to them, 'Do you know what I have done to you? You call me Teacher and Lord - and you are right, for that is what I am. So if I, your Lord and Teacher, have washed your feet, you also ought to wash one another's feet. For I have set you an example, that you also should do as I have done to you.

John 13: 12-15

At the last supper Jesus instituted the Eucharist, blessing bread and wine and inviting his disciples to do the same in memory of him. He also stooped down to wash their feet, drawing an explicit link between the Eucharist and the act of service. In his encyclical *Deus caritas est*, Pope Benedict reminds us that a Eucharist which does not lead us to undertake concrete acts of love is a fragmented one; robbed, as it were, of everything that it can be for us. Here our willingness to be fed on the body and blood of Christ, our readiness to receive the Word of God in Scripture, our recognition of the presence of Christ in others and our openness to the transforming power of the Holy Spirit is crucial.

Unless we want to be fed how will we come to understanding? Unless we seek to understand how will we know how to love? Unless we are open to the working of the Holy Spirit, who explains and transforms, how will we be able to love?

From Pope Benedict XVI's address at World Youth Day, Sydney 2008

At each Mass, in fact, the Holy Spirit descends anew, invoked by the solemn prayer of the Church, not only to transform our gifts of bread and wine into the Lord's body and blood, but also to transform our lives, to make us, in his power, 'one body, one spirit in Christ'.

My God, I love Thee above all things,
and in all things, with my whole soul,
because Thou art worthy of all love!

St. Alphonsus Liguori (1696 - 1787)

Good Friday

But when they came to Jesus and saw that he was already dead, they did not break his legs. Instead, one of the soldiers pierced his side with a spear, and at once blood and water came out.

John 19:33-34

Every Good Friday it is John's account of the Passion that we listen to. Uniquely, John's Gospel recounts the piercing of Christ's side and the outpouring of blood and water. In the liturgy the mingling of water and wine at the preparation of the gifts is a reminder of this. Here the priest prays, 'through the mystery of this water and wine may we come to share in the divinity of Christ who humbled himself to share in our humanity'. Water, as we have seen in our meditation on the Woman at the Well, is a metaphor for the Holy Spirit (Thursday of week 4). It is through the suffering of Christ and the work of the Holy Spirit, which poured forth from the Cross and at Pentecost, that we are reconciled to God, by the Son, in the power of the Spirit.

Soul of Christ, sanctify me.
Body of Christ, heal me.
Blood of Christ, drench me.
Water from the side of Christ, wash me.
Passion of Christ, strengthen me.
Good Jesus, hear me.
In your wounds, shelter me.
From turning away keep me.
From the evil one protect me.
At the hour of my death call me.
Into your presence lead me,
to praise you with all your saints
for ever and ever.
Amen.

Anima Christi, Thanksgiving after Mass; early 14th century

Holy Saturday

If the Spirit of him who raised Jesus from the dead dwells in you, he who raised Christ from the dead will give life to your mortal bodies also through his Spirit that dwells in you.

Romans 8:11

As we rejoice in Christ's victory over sin and death, we rejoice too, that his being raised from the dead is a victory we are invited to share in. It is towards this victory, this most precious of gifts, that the Lord, the Giver of Life, who lives in us and who is the source of every gift, will lead us.

To him who searches the depths of God,
who leads us into all knowledge and truth,
who is one with the Father and the Son,
be glory
for ever and ever.
Amen.

Renewal of Baptismal Promises

Do you reject sin,
so as to live in the freedom of God's children?
I do.

Do you reject the glamour of evil,
and refuse to be mastered by sin?
I do.

Do you reject Satan,
father of sin and prince of darkness?
I do.

Do you believe in God, the Father almighty,
creator of heaven and earth?
I do.

Do you believe in Jesus Christ, his only Son, our Lord,
who was born of the Virgin Mary,
was crucified, died, and was buried, rose from the dead,
and is now seated at the right hand of the Father?
I do.

Do you believe in the Holy Spirit,
the holy catholic Church, the communion of saints,
the forgiveness of sins, the resurrection of the body,
and life everlasting?
I do.

God, the all-powerful Father of our Lord Jesus Christ,
has given us a new birth by water and the Holy Spirit,
and forgiven all our sins.

May God also keep us faithful to our Lord Jesus Christ
for ever and ever.
Amen.